splatter

JANICE MARRIOTT

photographs by Sarah Hunter

LEARNING
MEDIA®

Distributed in the United States of America by Pacific Learning,
P. O. Box 2723, Huntington Beach, CA 92647-0723
Web site: www.pacificlearning.com

Published 1999 by Learning Media Limited,
Box 3293, Wellington 6001, New Zealand
Web site: www.learningmedia.com

10 9 8 7 6 5 4

Printed in Hong Kong

ISBN 0 478 22951 8

PL 9315

Chapter 1

Sol and I are getting closer and closer … and I'm getting scared.

But Greg knows what he's doing. All of his family ride quad bikes. He's been riding all his life, but I haven't even been close to one before. I shouldn't have said I'd come all the way out here. I should have stayed home, in front of the TV.

Help! We're at the door and …

… look at those bikes! One, two, three … four quads! I thought I was going for a quiet ride with Greg's grandfather, but they've got other ideas. Greg's going to show me what to do, and his grandfather's going to keep back out of the way.

It gets worse. Greg's friend, Sol, is riding with us too. He's probably an ace rider.

I don't think I'm up to this. Now I'm scared *and* worried.

"These bikes look like Mars buggies," I try to joke.

"No way," says Greg. "There's no water on Mars."

"So?"

"Where we're going, there's serious mud."

"Mud?"

"Yeah. It's a *little* bit muddy."

Greg and Sol laugh.

I think they're joking. The bikes look clean. There's no mud in sight.

We go into the shed. All kinds of wet-weather clothing is hanging around the walls. "First you put this special gear on," Greg says.

I look at the blue pants.

"Why?" I ask.

"Because of the mud," he says.

Sol grabs a pair of camouflage pants. Greg picks bright red ones. "Hey!" I think. "This is a race. The winner gets the best gear!" I'm way behind the others because I forget to take my boots off first and I get all tangled up.

Sol gets the jacket with yellow stripes down the sleeves. Greg gets the bright red pants. These guys are fast, and we haven't started biking yet.

But there's no going back now, not with Sol and Greg looking at me. Do I really need these gloves? They're as big as catcher's mitts. I'm ready, and I look really weird.

Greg sticks his thumb on the bike's accelerator. Then he shows me where the foot brake is, on the right-hand side. He tells me that the foot brake stops both back wheels, and the lever on the handlebar works on the front wheels.

"Most of the time you just use the hand brake," he says.

"Yeah. I can do this. It's easy," I say, to make myself feel good.

Then Greg shows me how to start the bike. "You just push this, and it goes."

"What about a clutch?" I ask, trying to sound as though I know all about engines.

"No clutch," he says. "Just the gears – five forward and one reverse. To change gear, you take your thumb off the accelerator, shift the gear lever with your foot, then speed up again."

I do the actions with my thumb and foot, to help me remember what he's saying.

He tells me that he checked the petrol before I arrived. "The tank holds enough gas to go a hundred miles," he says.

"We're not going that far!"

"No. Just a short, easy ride today. You'll be fine," he says as he checks the bikes.

I just stand there. My dream is really going to happen. It *is* happening. I'm going to ride a four-wheeler. It's a strange feeling.

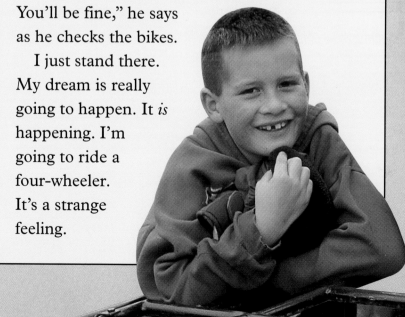

Then I get on. Now that I'm sitting in position, Greg shows me everything again. The bike's not moving, I'm just feeling the controls, and it feels good. Just when I'm all ready to go, Greg disappears into the shed again and comes out with the helmets!

Chapter 2

"Not helmets! There's no one here. We don't need them," I say. But Greg says we're not going anywhere until I'm wearing one. So here goes.

This helmet is massive! I feel like I'm going on a moon mission. But now we're ready to roll. This is the moment my dream ride starts. I'm nervous and excited all at once.

"To drive off," says Greg, "just squeeze the lever on the handlebar – that releases the brake."

I do what he says.

The bike starts quietly, and I squeeze the accelerator through my huge gloves. I go forward, nice and slowly.

We drive to a field to practice. "Turn off the engine," Greg says. "You've got to learn to brake, to accelerate, to change gears, and to use the horn. We don't go anywhere until you've got them all right."

So Sol and I practice, over and over again. We start the engines, drive round the daffodils, then put the brakes on. We're learning stopping, starting, and steering. Greg stands close by, in case I do something stupid. But I'm not going to. I can do this. This is cool!

We drive back to the shed, and Greg's granddad ties a shovel onto the bike.

"Why do we need that?" I ask.

"It's good to have it, just in case," his grandfather says.

"In case of what?" I wonder.

We head off into the unknown! I'm the last –
except for Greg's grandfather. He's "tail end
Charlie" today. He says he'll keep an eye on us
but not get in the way. The track's bumpy, but
it's nothing I can't handle.

Hey! Where's Greg taking us!

Chapter 3

We're deep in something that looks like jungle. Plants with sharp edges hang over the bikes. Suddenly I'm glad of the special clothes, and the gloves and helmet.

I'm so busy looking around that I get stuck. The mud sucks at my wheels. There's no way I can get out of this, so Greg gets off his bike and jumps onto mine. He drives it out of the muck. That guy is a great rider.

Off we go again! The bikes are really quiet.
They each have an air-cooled motorbike engine
with two huge mufflers. That's unusual – even
cars have only one muffler. They made the
bikes that way at first because they were farm
bikes. The farmers didn't want the noise to
scare the animals. Sol tells me that if you stand
ten feet away from the bike, you can hardly
hear the engine running.

The track gets narrower and stickier.

"Hey, Greg," I yell, "we aren't going into anything more difficult than this, are we?"

"You just wait," he says.

One moment we're rolling along, enjoying it, and the next, it's Sol's turn to hit trouble. He  gets stuck in a rut so deep his tire won't go over it. The tire's spinning. Sol's shouting. Mud's flying. Splatter!

Splatter

Splatter!

Greg gets off his bike again and unties the
shovel. His boots suck in the mud. Squelch! He
doesn't look so clean any more. Neither do the
bikes. He levels out the ground so that the tires
can go over it. "See," he says. "Nothing to it."

"You mean, we keep going?"

"You bet!"

That means I
have to go over
the same rut.
Would I make it?
Careful … slow
… go!

Yeah! I'm over. "Nothing can be worse than that," I think.

Greg laughs. "Next stop, the water bog!"

Chapter 4

We turn a corner, and ahead of us is a sheet of brown water. That's bad.

And it looks like we're going to drive through it. *Very bad!*

Sol goes first, pushing a huge wave of water in front of him. He gets stuck, of course, and Greg and I have to push him out.

This is fun. You don't have to be a brilliant rider. You just have to be steady. Greg's grandfather stays right out of the way and lets us get on with it.

The water hits the exhaust of the bike in front of me. It sizzles on the hot metal and showers off in a fine spray. My turn next. I plow in and churn through the really thick mud.

When we're all through the water bog, we stop for a rest. The engines are steaming because they're so hot. Am I glad I've got those gloves on!

I'm having great fun now. I can handle the puddles, no problem. This is better than my dream! I bet I don't get stuck again.

Chapter 5

I'm sloshing along, on a muddy track.

I look at my clothes. They're covered in mud. I look at the bikes. They're covered in mud too. Even the plants are covered in mud. It's the stickiest mud I've ever seen. It reminds me of melted chocolate. I start to get hungry.

Next thing, I'm bogged down again, because I was thinking about cookies and not the mud.

Sol and Greg help me out. I stand there and pose in the center of the giant puddle. This is something I'm never going to forget. I am the total mud man! So is Sol. So is Greg. Mud is everywhere!

"Hey," I yell, "I'm hungry!" We get back on our bikes and roll into a clearing. We get off and rest. Greg tells me that sometimes he brings a pizza wrapped up in newspaper. It keeps nice and warm in the space under the bike seat. Pizza! I can't wait!

Greg turns a lever and the seat comes off. Yes! There really is newspaper in there. I wait. I watch. Will the pizza have cheese and salami? Greg unwraps it. He's teasing me. It's just a bundle of paper.

After the break, we get back on the bikes. I'm not sure I can do much more pushing and hauling. I look at Greg. He looks at Sol. They both look at me.

"You've done all the hard parts, Darryl. Relax. How about a bit of cruising?"

We power on, and then I see it, a series of nice, shallow puddles. Just the thing for some easy, crazy water play. We size it up. Then we go straight through and out the other side. This is the ultimate.

We charge back and forward, with spray
winging up on both sides of us. I'm leading
now, which is brilliant. Sol's next, then
Greg. I love it when I hit the water, and
when we go through close together. Greg
gets the wettest because he collects the
spray from all the bikes. He seems to like it.

I'm getting good. I try standing to balance the bike. Greg watches and yells out instructions. No one wants to tip over. We try to do the biggest splashes. We're all so wet, we couldn't get any wetter if we tried.

Round the next corner, the road turns into boring, dry **gravel**. Then I stop.

"Hey, Greg, we don't have to go back the way we came, do we?"

He looks at Sol, and they wink at each other. A drip of mud springs off Greg's eyelashes.

"Follow me," he says.

I don't think I can keep this up any more.

We turn the next corner, and there is the other end of the daffodil field. We've been in a circle!

"I can't tell whether you liked it or not, with that helmet on," Greg says.

I slowly take my gloves off, then my helmet. I try to look serious, but the grin won't stop wiggling all over my face.

Chapter 6

We spend a while looking at the mud on the bikes, then the big clean up begins. We pull out a hose and turn it on. That mud just slides off the bikes.

Then Greg gets a cloth to wash the helmets.

We stretch our aching arms and legs. Sol looks at me. I look at him. We grab the hose and start a water fight with Greg.

I hope Greg's granddad will praise me for my riding skills. Instead, he says he's really pleased with Greg's teaching skills. But he says I can come again, for a day trip next time.

"Do you take food?" I ask.

He laughs. "You'll have to wait and find out." This is just the sort of answer that Greg would give.

"I'll bring a pizza," I say.